COOKING

Maltese Cuisine

Valerie

PUBLICATIONS

Publishers Enterprises Group (PEG) Ltd

Published by
Publishers Enterprises Group (PEG) Ltd,
P.E.G. Building, UB7 Industrial Estate,
San Ġwann SGN 09, Malta

http: //www.peg.com.mt
e-mail: contact@peg.com.mt

First printed in this format, 2001

ISBN: 99909-0-271-2

Printed in Malta by P.E.G. Ltd, San Ġwann

To my children
Miguel, Jean Pierre,
Jeanine and Charelle

Foreword

The need for a book dealing with Maltese recipes has long been felt. The dishes contained in this book are simple and easy to follow. They form part of the Maltese way-of-life and they are a tradition in themselves.

Maltese food is varied, adventurous and colourful. It reflects the character and mood of the Maltese people. It is uncomplicated, straight-forward and inviting, like the inhabitants of Malta.

My intentions in writing this book was to primarily invite visitors to our country to try out Maltese recipes in the quiet of their private kitchens. Nowadays, most big, supermarkets sell a wide selection of spices, herbs and other ingredients which make it easier to prepare the dishes described in this book.

My wish is that this book would be of help to our visitors and that they would relish and enjoy Maltese food and experiment with it when they leave Malta, thus carrying the memory of Malta in their hearts.

Valerie

Contents

SWEETS

Soups

LOCAL VEGETABLE SOUP
(MINESTRA)

Serves 4

Ingredients

2 onions
4 potatoes
4 tomatoes
¾ litre water
Knob of butter
1 tablespoon tomato paste

400g pumpkin
200g white pumpkin
Small cauliflower
Small cabbage
3 turnips (khol rabi)
200g pasta (maccaroni)

Method

Wash and chop all vegetables; put in a saucepan and add the water. Bring to the boil and simmer until all the vegetables are tender. Add the salt, pepper, butter, tomato paste and the pasta. Cook until the pasta is well done.

BEAN SOUP
(SOPPA TAL-FAŻOLA)

Serves 4

Ingredients

3 slices bacon
200g baked or boiled beans
½ litre water
1 tablespoon flour

1 tablespoon butter
Salt and pepper
Paprika

Method

Cook the bacon and add to the beans. Add cold water and cook until beans are soft, then rub through a strainer. Place on the fire and add a little more water if needed, as the soup must not be too thick. Blend in the flour and butter. Cook for a further 2 or 3 minutes. Season with salt, a dash of pepper and paprika.

WIDOW'S SOUP
(SOPPA TA' L-ARMLA)

Serves 4

Ingredients

2 carrots (chopped)
2 onions (chopped)
2 lettuces
400g peas
400g rikotta (cottage cheese)

50g butter
4 eggs
3 fresh soft cheese
¾ litre water

Method

Put the butter in a saucepan and saute all the vegetables until golden brown. Add the water and bring to the boil. Add the rikotta, soft cheeses and the eggs one at a time. Care must be taken not to break the rikotta, cheese and eggs.

TRIPE SOUP
(KIRXA)

Serves 4

Ingredients

1 kilo tripe
1 large khol rabi
1 onion
1 cauliflower
400g pumpkin

200g tomatoes
1 cabbage
6 potatoes
¾ litre water
Parsley to garnish

Method

Thorougly clean the tripe by scraping the insides to remove all fuzz. Rub with salt and wash well under running water. Cut into pieces and simmer for about 2 hours until the tripe is tender.

Wash and chop all vegetables and put in a pan with the water together with the tripe. Bring to the boil, add seasoning and cook until all vegetables are tender. Serve hot with grated parmesan cheese and parsley to garnish.

JERUSALEM ARTICHOKE SOUP
(SOPPA TAL-QAQOĊĊ)

Serves 4

Ingredients

¾kg Jerusalem artichokes
½ litre water
¼ teaspoon vinegar
Seasoning

50g butter
15g flour
150ml milk
Paprika pepper to garnish

Method

Wash, peel and chop the artichokes. Put into a saucepan with the water, vinegar and seasoning. Simmer gently for 30 minutes. Rub through a sieve, then return the purée to the saucepan together with the butter. Blend the flour with the cold milk, stir into the boiling purée and continue cooking, stirring all the time, until you have a smooth thick sauce. Garnish with paprika pepper.

CARROT AND TOMATO SOUP
(SOPPA TAT-TADAM U KARROTTI)

Serves 4

Ingredients

50g butter
1 small onion (chopped)
200g carrots
400g ripe tomatoes

Chopped parsley
1 teaspoon sugar
1 teaspoon salt and pepper
¾ litre water

Method

Melt the butter. Add the onion and cook for 2 or 3 minutes over low heat. Add the carrots and tomatoes roughly cut into pieces together with the sugar and seasonings. Stir all well together and add half the water. Bring to the boil, then simmer with the lid on the saucepan for approximately 10 minutes. Pour the rest of the water and bring to the boil. Garnish with chopped parsley.

GREEN PEA SOUP
(SOPPA TAL-PIŻELLI)

Serves 4

Ingredients

¼ litre stock
¼ litre water
200g green peas
1 celery stalk
1 onion
1 turnip

2 sprigs mint
1 tablespoon flour
1 tablespoon butter
Salt and pepper
Sugar

Method

Reserve half the amount of the green peas; to the stock and water add the rest of the peas, the celery stalk, the onion and turnip (cut into pieces), and the mint. Stew until the mass is tender. Strain through a sieve or coarse cheese-cloth. Add stock or water, if necessary; blend with the mixture of flour and butter, season with salt, pepper and a little sugar. Add the rest of the whole peas, cook for a few minutes and serve.

LENTIL SOUP
(SOPPA TA' L-GHADZ)

Serves 4

Ingredients

200g lentils
1 onion
1 tablespoon chopped parsley
4 tablespoons olive oil

1 clove crushed garlic
400g tomatoes
1¾ litre water
Seasonings

Method

Prior to the actual cooking of this soup, one must boil the lentils in salted water for about 1 hour. Strain the lentils and retain the water, add the parsley, onion and garlic. Bring to the boil and add the oil. Cook for a further 10 minutes; then add the strained tomatoes, salt and pepper and the lentils. Cook for another 20 minutes and serve hot.

MARROWS AND ONIONS SOUP

(SOPPA TAL-QARA' BAGHLI U BASAL)

Serves 4

Ingredients

3 small potatoes
2 large onions
400g rikotta (cottage cheese)
400g peas

400g marrows
50g butter
Salt and pepper

Method

Thoroughly wash all vegetables; after peeling and chopping the potatoes, onions and marrows, melt the butter and add the vegetables. Add the water and cook on a slow fire until the vegetables are well done. Add salt and pepper. Pass the vegetables through a passe purée or liquidizer. Reheat and simmer together with the cottage cheese for about 5 to 10 minutes.

VEGETABLE SOUP WITH MEAT
(KAWLATA)

Serves 4

Ingredients

¾ kilo pork
400g pumpkin
200g white pumpkin
Small cauliflower
Small cabbage
3 turnips (khol rabi)

2 onions
4 potatoes (whole)
4 tomatoes
¾ litre water
Knob of butter
1 tablespoon tomato soup

Method

After chopping all the vegetables (except the potatoes) put them in a saucepan with the water and bring to the boil. Add the meat and the rest of the ingredients and cook well. Serve the meat as a separate dish together with the potatoes. Some lemon juice would enrich the taste of the meat.

BEAN AND PASTA SOUP

(KUSKSU BIL-FUL)

Serves 4

Ingredients

*1 kilo green beans
  (either fresh or dried)
2 onions (chopped)
50g butter
100g tomato paste*

*100g pasta
  (the small beady type)
¾ litre water
Salt and pepper*

Method

Heat the butter and lightly saute the onions. When these attain a golden hue, add the water, salt and pepper. Bring the mass to the boil and add the tomato paste and the beans. Cook over a gentle heat until the beans are tender. Serve piping hot with some grated cheese to garnish.

Note: If the dried type of bean is being used, the beans should be peeled and soaked overnight in water.

POTATO SOUP
(SOPPA TAL-PATATA)

Serves 4

Ingredients

800g potatoes
1 onion
1-2 sticks of celery
50g fat
¾ litre water
Salt and pepper

1 bay leaf
25g flour
125ml milk
Chopped parsley
1 tablespoon evaporated milk
    or single cream

Method

Peel and slice the potatoes and chop the onion and celery. Melt the fat and saute the vegetables in it for 5 to 10 minutes. Add the liquid, seasoning and herbs. Bring to the boil and simmer till the vegetables are tender and the potatoes break up. Sieve or mash well with a potato masher, stir in the flour, blended to a smooth cream with the milk and allow to boil for a further 5 minutes. Add the chopped parsley and cream just before serving.

FISH SOUP
(ALJOTTA)

Serves 4

Ingredients

1 kilo small fish
   (bogue or mackerel)
1 onion
100g rice
1 clove of crushed garlic
3 tablespoons olive oil

Seasoning
1 bay leaf
Sprig of mint
200g tomatoes (chopped)
1 litre water

Method

Fry the onion and garlic over a gentle heat. Add the chopped tomatoes, the herbs and the water. Bring to the boil and then add the fish. Cook over a slow fire until the fish is tender. Strain the fish soup and clean the fish of its bones. Return to the pan, adding the cleaned rice, cooking until the rice is tender. Serve with a dash of lemon juice.

Sauces

TOMATO SAUCE
(ZALZA TAD-TADAM)

Ingredients

Bay leaf
15g flour
300ml water
Salt and pepper
Pinch of sugar

25g butter
1 onion (chopped)
1 carrot (chopped)
1 rasher bacon (chopped)
6 large fresh tomatoes

Method

Heat the butter and cook the onion, carrot and bacon for a few minutes. Add tomatoes, bay leaf and simmer for 10 minutes. Blend the flour with the water, add to the ingredients and simmer gently for about 30 minutes. Stir from time to time. Add seasoning and sugar.

CURRY SAUCE
(ZALZA BIL-CURRY)

Ingredients
salt
1 level tablespoon cornflour
300ml water
1 dessertspoon chutney

1 onion
1 green pepper
25g butter
1 level tablespoon curry
    powder

Method
Chop the onion and pepper and saute in the butter. Add curry powder, salt and cornflour. Stir until blended, cook for a few minutes and add the water. Bring to the boil, stirring all the time. Add the chutney. Cover and simmer for at least one hour.

WHITE SAUCE
(ZALZA BAJDA)

Ingredients

25g butter or margerine
25g flour

300ml milk
Salt and pepper

Method

Heat the butter or margerine, remove from the heat and stir in the flour. Return to the heat and cook for a further few minutes taking care that the mixture does not brown.

Remove from the heat and gradually blend in the cold milk. Bring to the boil and cook, stirring with a wooden spoon, until smooth and thick; season well.

CAPER SAUCE
(ZALZA BAJDA BIL-KAPPAR)

Follow the recipe as for the Basic White Sauce and add 2 teaspoons capers and a little caper vinegar when the sauce has thickened.

CHEESE SAUCE
(ZALZA BAJDA BIL-ĠOBON)

Follow the recipe for the Basic White Sauce, then add 100g grated cheese when sauce has thickened. One can also add a little mustard.

TOMATO SAUCE WITH EGGS AND RIKOTTA
(FRAKASIJA)

Serves 4

Follow recipe for tomato sauce. Reheat, add 4 eggs (taking care that they do not break). Add 400g of rikotta and a tin of peas. Cook over a slow fire until the eggs are rather hard. Serve with chips and salad.

PIQUANT SAUCE
(ZALZA PIKKANTI)

Ingredients

2 tablespoons capers
2 tablespoons meat stock
150ml vinegar
6 tablespoons water
½ teaspoon freshly ground
   black pepper
½ teaspoon tomato paste
½ teaspoon mustard

2 tablespoons butter
2 onions
2 carrots
thyme
1 tablespoon chopped parsley
1 clove garlic
2 tablespoons flour

Method

Melt the fat and slice into it the onions and carrots. Add the thyme, parsley and garlic. When the carrot has softened, blend in the flour; add the stock, vinegar, water, tomato paste and mustard. Bring to the boil and add the pepper and capers. Simmer on gentle heat for at least one hour.

TOMATO AND EGG SAUCE
(BALBULJATA)

Serves 4

Follow recipe for tomato sauce. When the sauce has thickened, let it stand for about half an hour, then add 4 eggs. Mingle the eggs with the sauce using a fork. Serve with salad and chips.

Pasta and rice

BAKED RICE
(ROSS IL-FORN)

Serves 4

Ingredients

200g long grain rice	3 rashers of bacon
1 bottle milk	200g rikotta
200g minced pork	4 eggs (well beaten)
200g minced beef	Seasoning

Method

Make tomato sauce by melting a little fat and adding 200g tomato paste and a spoonful of sugar together with 150ml of water. Let the sauce cool. Grease a baking dish with fat and place the uncooked rice in it. Add the milk, sauce, meat, rikotta and the well beaten eggs. Stir well and add the seasoning. Bake in a moderate oven for about 45 minutes.

RAVIOLI
(RAVJUL)

Serves 4

Ingredients

Pastry:
100g flour
100g semolina
Some chilled salted
   water

Filling:
200g rikotta (cottage cheese)
2 well beaten eggs
2 tablespoonfuls
   finely chopped parsley
Pinch of salt

Method

Sift the flour and combine with the semolina. Gradually add the salted water and knead to form a rather stiff dough. Let it stand for half an hour. Mix the rikotta with the well beaten eggs, add parsley and salt.

Roll out pastry with thin long strips. Place spoonfuls of the rikotta mixture on the lower part of the strips. Fold over the upper part and press edges together taking care to cover the rokotta mixture. Cut the ravioli separately and place on a floured baking sheet.

Bring a large pan of salted water to the boil and place the ravioli one by one. Care must be taken not to break the ravioli when stirring. Let the ravioli boil until they float to the top. Drain well and serve with tomato sauce and grated cheese.

SPAGHETTI WITH AUBERGINES
(SPAGHETTI BIL-BRINĠIEL)

Serves 4

Ingredients

400g spaghetti
Tomato sauce
200g minced beef

200g minced pork
400g aubergines (sliced)
Seasoning

Method

Make the tomato sauce as for baked rice. Add the meat. Fry the aubergine slices until tender. Boil the spaghetti in salted water for about 12 minutes. Drain and serve the spaghetti topped with the sauce and slices of aubergine.

TARJA WITH BUTTER AND RIKOTTA
(TARJA BIL-BUTIR U R-RIKOTTA)

Serves 4

Ingredients

400g tarja or spaghetti

400g rikotta

100g grated parmesan cheese

100g butter

Seasoning

Method

Boil the pasta in salted water for about 12 minutes. Drain and transfer to a warmed dish, stirring in the butter, cheese, rikotta and seasoning. Serve piping hot.

Note: Tarja is a local pasta which is like very fine thin spaghetti.

RICE WITH CHICKEN LIVERS
(ROSS BIL-FWIED TAT-TIĠIEĠ)

Serves 4

Ingredients

400g chicken livers
200g boiled rice
4 large onions (chopped)
100g butter

3 tablespoons caraway seeds
1 teaspoon mixed spice
100g peas
Seasoning

Method

Melt the fat and fry the chopped onions until golden brown. Add the chicken livers and cook over a slow fire. Add the spice, the seasoning, the caraway seeds and the peas. In another pan, melt some butter and fry the boiled rice for a few minutes. Add the chicken liver mixture and mix well.

STUFFED PASTA SHELLS
(INJOKKI MIMLIJA)

Serves 4

Ingredients

400g pasta shells
Tomato sauce
200g minced pork
200g minced beef
3 rashers bacon (chopped)

100g rikotta
4 well beaten eggs
Seasoning
Grated cheese

Method

Boil the pasta shells until half-cooked and drain. Make tomato sauce as for baked rice. Combine the meat with the rikotta and the well beaten eggs. Add seasoning and fill each pasta shell with the rikotta mixture. Place the shells in a greased oven dish and cover with the tomato paste and grated cheese. Bake in a moderate oven for about 30 minutes.

TIMPANA
(TIMPANA)

Serves 4

Ingredients

200g minced beef
200g minced pork
4 eggs (well beaten)
2 hard boiled eggs
100g grated cheese
200g rikotta
4 tablespoons evaporated milk
Salt and pepper

100g tomato paste
Knob of fat
Spoonful of sugar
150ml heated water
400g flaky pastry
400g macaroni
200g chicken liver (chopped)
200g bacon (chopped)

Method

Sauce: Heat the fat, add the tomato paste and the water; then add the sugar. Stir until the sauce has thickened. Toss in the chopped chicken livers and bacon plus the minced beef and pork. Simmer for at least 10 minutes.

Macaroni: Fill a large pot with water, add a spoonful of kitchen salt and bring to the boil. Add a teaspoonful of oil to prevent the macaroni from sticking together. Toss in the pasta and cook over a rapid fire until the macaroni are nearly cooked. Drain well and mix with the sauce mixture.

In a separate container, beat the eggs, add the grated cheese, evaporated milk, salt and pepper and rikotta. Blend this mixture with the sauce and macaroni, adding the chopped hard boiled eggs.

Finally grease an oven dish with butter and line the bottom and sides with the flaky pastry. Place the macaroni in the dish, cover with the remaining pastry, pierce the top and bake until golden brown.

BAKED MACARONI
(IMQARRUN FIL-FORN)

Follow recipe as for Timpana but omit the pastry.

Pies

MEAT PIE
(TORTA TAL-LAHAM)

Serves 4

Ingredients

200g kidneys (chopped)
200g beef (minced)
200g pork (minced)
100g bacon (chopped)
200g peas

4 large onions (chopped)
1 teaspoon mixed spice
1 teaspoon curry
Seasoning
400g puff pastry

Method

Fry the onions in some fat until tender. Add the kidneys, beef, pork and bacon. Simmer for 10 minutes. Add the spice, curry, seasoning and peas. Cook for a further 10 minutes. Line an oven dish with the pastry, place the filling and cover with the pastry. Pierce the top and cook for about 50 minutes in a hot oven.

TUNA PIE
(TORTA TAT-TONN)

Serves 4

Ingredients

*500g fresh tuna or two large
tins of tinned tuna
100g green olives
4 large tomatoes
2 green peppers*

*1 aubergine
1 small cauliflower
1 large onion
400g puff pastry*

Method

If fresh tuna is being used, fry the fish in oil. Remove bones. In a large saucepan cook the tomatoes, green peppers, aubergine, cauliflower and onion in some vegetable oil. Add the tuna, green olives and seasoning.

Grease an oven dish with some fat, line the bottom and sides with the pastry and place the filling. Cover with pastry and cook until golden brown.

PIGEON PIE
(TORTA TAL-BĊIEĊEN)

Serves 4

Ingredients

4 pigeons
400g potatoes (mashed)
200g carrots
200g leeks
4 onions

200g butter
3 tablespoons flour
600ml dry wine
300ml water
400g puff pastry

Method

Clean pigeons. Heat butter and brown the whole pigeons. Remove from heat and in the same butter fry the carrots, leeks and onions. Add the flour, and gradually pour in the wine and water. Remove the bones from the pigeons and add the meat to the vegetable mass. Line an oven dish with the pastry, place the mashed potatoes at the bottom and pour the pigeon mixture. Cover with pastry, pierce the top and bake in a hot oven until golden brown. Serve hot.

MALTESE CHEESE PIE
(TORTA TAR-RIKOTTA)

Serves 4

Ingredients

3 eggs
200g rikotta (cottage cheese)
50g cooked peas
25g parsley (chopped)

¼ teaspoon chopped
  White pepper
½ teaspoon mixed dried herbs
400g puff pastry
Beaten egg for glazing

Method

Whisk the eggs and add the rikotta, peas, parsley, salt, pepper and herbs. Roll out half the pastry to line a 15cm flan ring or dish. Pour in filling, brush edges with beaten egg and cover with the remaining pastry. Trim and pinch edges together, pierce with a fork to allow steam to escape and decorate with pastry leaves made from the trimmings. Brush with beaten egg. Bake in a hot oven for 15-20 minutes, reduce the heat to moderate when the top is risen and golden and cook for a further 30 minutes. Serve hot or cold.

LAMPUKI PIE
(TORTA TAL-LAMPUKI)

Serves 4

Ingredients

800g lampuki
3 onions
400g tomatoes
2 kilos spinach
(previously boiled)
100g tomato paste

100g chopped olives
50g capers
Mint
Seasoning
400g puff pastry

Method

Clean the fish, cut into slices and roll in seasoned flour. Fry in hot oil, remove bones. Chop onions, and fry in the same oil, add the tomatoes and simmer for 10 minutes. Add the other ingredients and cook on a slow fire for a further half hour. Add the fish and line a greased oven dish with the pastry, place the fish mixture and cover with pastry. Pierce the top and bake in a moderate oven until golden brown. Serve hot.

RABBIT PIE
(TORTA TAL-FNIEK)

Serves 4

Ingredients
1 young rabbit
150ml red wine
50g tomato paste
400g peas

4 onions
1 bay leaf
400g puff pastry

Method
Chop the rabbit and marinate it in the wine for about 1½ hours. Melt some lard and fry the chopped onions until golden brown. Add rabbit and fry on a gentle heat. Pour the wine and the tomato paste. Stir well. Add the bay leaf and the peas. Simmer until the rabbit is tender. Remove from heat and clean the cooked rabbit of all its bones. Mix the rabbit meat with the rest of the stew. Line an oven dish with the pastry, pour in the filling and cover with pastry. Pierce the top. Bake in a hot oven until golden brown. Serve hot.

CHEESE CAKES
(PASTIZZI TAR-RIKOTTA)

Serves 4-6

Ingredients

3 eggs

200g rikotta (cottage cheese)

¼ teaspoon salt

White pepper

200g puff pastry

Method

Preheat the oven to hot 425°F or gas mark 7 (220°C). Whisk eggs in a large basin. Press the rikotta through a sieve and mix well. Add the salt and pepper. Roll out the pastry into long strip and cut into squares. Put a tablespoonful of the filling in the centre and bring together the corners of the pastry. Place the cheese cakes on a baking sheet and cook for 45 minutes. Serve hot.

PEAS PASTIES
(QASSATAT TAL-PIŻELLI)

Serves 4-6

Ingredients
200g short crust pastry
1 large onion
50g butter

400g cooked peas
Salt and pepper

Method
Cook the chopped onion in the butter. Add the cooked peas. Mix well. Roll out the pastry cut into rounds the size of a tea plate. Place a pile of the filling in the centre and brush the pastry edge with water. Pick up the edges and seal together at the top leaving a round hole at the top. Bake in a hot oven for about 45 minutes.

ANCHOVY PASTIES
(QASSATAT TA' L-INĊOVA)

Follow the method for the Peas Pasties substituting the peas for 200g crushed anchovy.

Meats

BEEFSTEAK WITH ONIONS
(ĊANGA BIL-BASAL)

Serves 4

Ingredients

1 kilo sirloin steak
50g butter or margarine
4 onions (sliced)

1 teaspoon salt
¼ teaspoon pepper
125ml boiling water

Method

Cut steak into four portions and flatten meat lightly. Melt 2 tablespoons of the fat in a pan. Add onions and fry until softened and brown. Remove onions and keep warm. Add remaining fat to pan and heat. Sprinkle meat with salt and pepper and fry each side for about 5 minutes. Remove meat. Pour boiling water into pan and stir. Place this gravy on the meat and serve the steaks garnished with onions.

BEEF OLIVES
(BRAĠOLI)

Ingredients

½ kilo steak
100g tomato purée
400g tomatoes
2 onions (chopped)
200g peas
125ml water

100g ham (chopped)
100g bacon (chopped)
200g pork (minced)
1 tablespoon parsley (chopped)
1 hard boiled egg (chopped)
Seasoning

Method

Make the tomato paste by frying the onion, add the tomatoes and tomato paste. Add the water and simmer for 30 minutes. Add the peas. Make beef olives by mixing the ham with the bacon, pork, parsley, hard boiled egg and seasoning. Lay the pieces of steak flat on the table, put some of the pork mixture in the middle, roll and secure with toothpicks or thread. Add to the tomato sauce and cook for a further 30 minutes. Serve the sauce with spaghetti and the beef olives as a separate dish with salad and chips.

STUFFED RUMP STEAK
(FALDA MIMLIJA)

Serves 4

Ingredients

*1 kilo rump or fillet steak
(whole piece with a
arting in the middle)
100g bacon
100g ham
1 hard boiled egg*

*200g minced pork
1 tablespoon parsley (chopped)
1 clove garlic
1 egg
1 carrot (chopped)
1 stalk celery*

Method

Mix together the bacon, ham, hard boiled egg, minced pork, parsley, garlic and bind with the egg. Put this mixture in the parting of the steak, secure with thread or toothpicks and place in a pan filled with water. When the water boils, add the chopped carrot, the celery stalk, salt and pepper. Simmer for about 1 hour and serve the broth as a separate dish. Serve the rump steak with salad and chips.

PIG'S TROTTERS IN SAUCE
(SAQAJN TAL-MAJJAL)

Serves 4

Ingredients

4 pig's trotters
1 large onion
1 slice bacon
1 bay leaf
Seasoning

2 spoonfuls butter
Chopped parsley
1 carrot (chopped)
1 tin peas

Method

Thoroughly clean the trotters. Place in a saucepan with the chopped onion and bacon. Cover with water, bring to the boil and skim. Add the rest of the ingredients and cook until the trotters are tender. Serve with salad and mashed potatoes.

CALF'S HEART STUFFED AND STEWED
(QLUB MIMLIJA)

Ingredients

1 calf's heart
1 tablespoon parsley (chopped)
1 tablespoon ham (chopped)
3 tablespoons bacon (chopped)
Seasoning
1 egg

2 large onions
100g tomato paste
125ml water
100g carrots
100g peas

Method

Clean the heart and soak in cold salted water for at least 30 minutes. Mix the chopped parsley with the ham, bacon, seasoning and egg. Stuff the heart with the mixture, secure with thread and toss into some seasoned flour. Melt some butter and brown the heart. Remove from heat and add the chopped onions. Add the tomato paste and water. Place the heart in the saucepan together with the carrots and peas. Simmer for at least one hour.

BAKED MEAT
(LAHAM IL-FORN)

Serves 4

Ingredients

1 kilo rump steak or pork
8 large potatoes
4 large onions
3 cloves garlic

50g butter
1 tablespoon parsley
125ml water
Salt and pepper

Method

Grease an oven dish with the butter, and place the onion rounds at the bottom. Place the sliced potatoes on the onions and put the meat at the centre. Cover with potatoes, add the garlic and parsley. Add the water, salt and pepper and bake in the centre of a moderately hot oven for 1½ hours.

BRAIN CAKES
(PULPETTI TAL-MOHH)

Serves 4

Ingredients
1 large pork brain
1 spoonful parsley (chopped)
Clove of garlic

3 well-beaten eggs
2 spoonfuls butter
Salt and pepper

Method
Mash the brain until quite soft. Add the well beaten eggs, parsley, garlic and seasoning. Melt the butter over moderate heat. Toss a spoonful of the brain mixture into some seasoned flour and fry the cakes in the butter. Put on some kitchen paper to rid off excess fat. Serve with salad and chips.

MEAT LOAF IN
PORK CAUL
(MAJJAL FIL-MINDIL)

Serves 4

Ingredients

200g beef (minced)
200g pork (minced)
100g ham
100g bacon
200g liver

1 spoon parsley
4 beaten eggs
400g whole pork caul
Salt and pepper

Method

Mix all ingredients together with the well beaten eggs. Place this mixture on to the caul. Roll into a long cake, place on a well greased oven dish and bake for about one hour. This meat loaf should be served cold with salad and chips.

RABBIT
COUNTRY STYLE
(FENEK LA KAMPANJOLA)

Serves 4

Ingredients

1 rabbit (cut into joints)
100g lard
1 large glass of red wine
4 large onions (chopped)

4 large tomatoes (chopped)
4 bay leaves
1 clove garlic

Method

Melt the lard and brown the rabbit joints. Add the chopped onions, tomatoes, bay leaves, garlic and wine. Cover and simmer until rabbit is tender. Serve with salad and chips.

BAKED RABBIT
(FENEK IL-FORN)

Serves 4

Ingredients

1 whole rabbit   ½ kilo onions (sliced)
100g lard   1 kilo potatoes (sliced)
1 large glass red wine

Method

Grease an oven dish with the lard, and place the sliced onions at
the bottom. Cover the onions with the sliced potatoes and place
the whole rabbit on top of the potatoes. Add the wine and some
water, and cook in a moderately hot oven until the rabbit is brown.

RABBIT STEW
(STUFFAT TAL-FENEK)

Serves 4-6

Ingredients

1 rabbit fried
50g lard
200g tomato paste
400g tomatoes (peeled)
50g sugar
200g peas
4 onions (chopped)

2 carrots (chopped)
2 bay leaves
1 glass red wine
Seasoning
½ teaspoon oregano
1 teaspoon mixed spices
300ml stock

Method

In a large heavy saucepan melt the lard, add the onion and cook, stirring occasionally for 8 minutes or until the onion is soft and translucent but not brown. Add the tomatoes and chopped carrots. Cook over a gentle heat for a further 10 minutes. Add the wine and the stock, the tomato purée and the sugar and stir well. Add the bay leaves, seasoning, and herbs and let the stew simmer for about an hour. Serve with spaghetti and the rabbit stew could be used as another separate dish.

LAMB STEW
(STUFFAT TAL-HARUF)

Serves 4

Ingredients
1 kilo lamb
4 cloves garlic
3 tablespoons butter
Oregano
Rosemary

1 glass red wine
50g tomato paste
4 large potatoes
100g peas
100g carrots (chopped)

Method
Fry the garlic in fat; add the herbs and the meat until the butter is brown. Reduce the heat and add the wine and the diluted tomato paste. Add the potatoes and simmer for 30 minutes adding enough boiling water to prevent the meat from drying. Add the peas and chopped carrots.

PORK CASSEROLE

(STUFFAT TAL-MAJJAL)

Serves 4-6

Ingredients

1 kilo pork	50g flour
25g lard	Seasoning
2 leeks (chopped)	250ml red wine
1 garlic clove (crushed)	Tabasco sauce
500g pork cut in cubes	100g peas

Method

Melt the lard in flameproof casserole, fry leeks and garlic for a few minutes.

Toss pork in seasoned flour, add the leeks and fry for 10 minutes. Add wine, seasoning and peas. Bring to the boil, cover and simmer for 30 minutes.

Place casserole in a moderately hot oven and bake for about 30 minutes.

QUAIL FRICASSEE
(STUFFAT TAS-SUMMIEN)

Serves 4

Ingredients
4 quails (cleaned and quartered)
3 large onions (finely chopped)
4 potatoes
100g butter
200g peas

4 carrots (chopped)
250ml stock
1 glass red wine
Salt and pepper
100g tomato paste

Method
Heat the butter and brown the quail. Add the onions and carrots and cook for 10 minutes. Add the stock and the diluted tomato paste. When it boils, lower the heat and add the wine, the seasoning and the halved potatoes, cook gently for a further 30 minutes.

PIGEON STEW
(STUFFAT TAL-BĊIEĊEN)

Serves 4

Ingredients
4 pigeons (cleaned and halved)
4 potatoes
4 carrots
6 small onions peeled
    and left whole
4 tomatoes peeled and cut

100g butter
1 teaspoon salt
½ teaspoon white pepper
250ml stock
200g peas
1 glass red wine

Method

Heat the butter and brown the pigeons. Remove from pan. Clean and chop all vegetables. Fry the small whole onions in same fat as for pigeons. Place the pigeons and onions in a pot, add the vegetables, salt, pepper and stock. Cook over high heat until the mass boils. Add the wine and the peas. Simmer gently for a further half hour.

LAND SNAILS WITH ARJOLI
(BEBBUX BL-ARJOLI)

Serves 4

Ingredients

2 kilos land snails
Salt

For the Arjoli:
1 tablespoon oil
1 tablespoon parsley (chopped)

150g bread crumbs
1 tablespoon garlic (mashed)
1 hot red pepper (chopped)
1 tablespoon vinegar
Pepper

Method

Wash the snails in fresh water to which 2½ tablespoonfuls of salt have been added.

Soak for 10 minutes.

Change water, add the salt and wash the snails for four times. Put in a large saucepan, cover with water and boil for about 1½ hours.

Make the arjoli by mixing well all the ingredients.

The snails should be served hot with the arjoli and any green salad.

STUFFED GREEN PEPPERS
(BŻAR AĦDAR MIMLI)

Serves 4

Ingredients
8 large green peppers
150g white bread
4 tablespoons milk
1 tablespoon parsley (chopped)

2 tablespoons tomato
  chutney
Salt and pepper
100g minced pork (fried)
Cooked long grain rice

Method
Cut off the top of the peppers, scoop out core and seeds and wash peppers. Drop into boiling water and cook for 3 minutes. Crumble the bread and soften with milk; add the parsley, chutney, salt, pepper and the pork. Fill the peppers with this mixture. Replace the tops and put into a baking tin with some water. Cook in a moderately hot oven for 35 minutes or until the peppers are soft. Serve on a bed of rice.

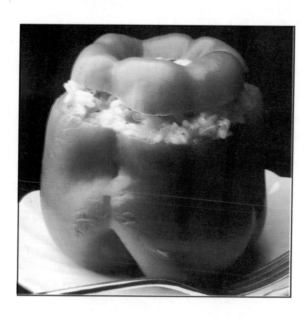

STUFFED GLOBE ARTICHOKES
(QAQOĊĊ MIMLI)

Serves 4

Ingredients

4 artichokes
4 tablespoons parsley (chopped)
150g breadcrumbs
100g anchovies (cut finely)

1 clove garlic (chopped)
6 olives (chopped)
Salt and pepper

Method

Soak artichokes in salted water, drain and flatten the leaves by beating the artichokes whilst it is upside down. Mix all ingredients and fill the artichokes with the mixture. Put in a saucepan and pour oil and vinegar on the artichokes. Fill the bottom of the pan with some water, cover and simmer for about 1½ hours or until the leaves can be easily pulled out. Serve hot with salad and fish.

STUFFED AUBERGINE
(BRINĠIEL MIMLI)

Serves 4

Ingredients
4 medium-sized aubergines
½ teaspoon salt
2 teaspoons butter
50g bacon (chopped)
1 tablespoon parsley (chopped)
1 tomato (skinned and chopped)

50g fresh breadcrumbs
Salt and pepper
1 tablespoon finely
   chopped cooked onion
200g minced pork
100g grated cheese

Method
Wash the aubergines, remove stalk and cut in half length-wise. Boil the aubergines and scoop out the flesh from the centre. Put the butter in a pan and add all the ingredients plus the scopped flesh of the aubergines.

Fill aubergine cases with stuffing an cook in a moderately hot oven for about one hour.

Serve hot with chips and salad.

STUFFED MARROW
(QARA' BAGHLI MIMLI)

Serves 4

Ingredients

1 kilo marrows
200g minced pork
100g bacon
1 tablespoon tomato paste
2 large onions
50g butter

Salt and pepper
¼ teaspoon curry
¼ teaspoon mixed spice
8 large potatoes (sliced)
2 onions (sliced)

Method

Cut the marrows in halves; boil for 5 minutes and scoop out the centre.

Grease an oven dish with fat, lay the sliced onions and potatoes at the bottom and prepare the filling. In a pan, brown the onions in the butter, add the minced pork, and the chopped bacon and simmer for 5 minutes. Add the scooped marrows tomato paste, salt, pepper and the spices. Fill the marrow halves with the meat mixture and bake in a moderate hot oven for about 1 hour.

Fish

GRILLED SWORDFISH
(PIXXISPAD MIXWI)

Serves 4

Ingredients

1 kilo swordfish
1 clove garlic
Mint

Juice of 1 lemon
Olive oil
Seasoning

Method

Prior to the cooking of the swordfish, marinate the slices of fish in the lemon juice and seasoning for 1 hour. Place the fish on a baking dish, add the garlic, mint and olive oil and grill in a slow oven for about 1 hour. Serve with salad and chips.

SWORDFISH
IN CAPER SAUCE
(PIXXISPAD FIZ-ZALZA TAL-KAPPAR)

Serves 4

Ingredients

1 kilo swordfish
100g tomato paste
½ kilo tomatoes

3 large onions
Seasoning
100g capers
Olive oil

Method

Heat the olive oil, add the sliced onions and cook until brown. Add the tomatoes and tomato paste and cook on a slow heat for 15 minutes. Add the capers and seasoning. In another saucepan, fry the swordfish and serve with the caper sauce, salad and chips.

POACHED GROUPER
(ĊERNA FL-IMBJANK)

Serves 4-6

Ingredients

1 whole grouper
4 tablespoons olive oil
2 cloves garlic

Parsley
Mint
Water

Method
Place the grouper in a fire-proof dish, add the olive oil, garlic, parsley, mint and half cover with water. Cook over a very gentle heat until the fish is tender. Care must be taken not to poach the fish rapidly otherwise the fish tend to break or become very dry. Serve the grouper with salad and chips.

GRILLED GROUPER WITH MUSTARD SAUCE
(ĊERNA BIL-MUSTARD SAUCE)

Serves 4-6

Ingredients

1 whole grouper
2 tablespoons olive oil
25g margerine

25g flour
150ml milk
1 teaspoon dry mustard

Method
Coat the grouper with the olive oil and grill until tender. Make the sauce by gently heating the margarine. Remove from the heat and stir in the flour and mustard. Return to the heat for a few minutes, stirring all the time. Remove from the heat and gradually blend in the cold milk. Bring to the boil and cook, stirring with a wooden spoon until smooth. Season well and place on the grouper. Serve with salad and chips.

BAKED STUFFED LAMPUKI
(LAMPUKI MIMLIJA L-FORN)

Serves 4

Ingredients

1 kilo lampuki
2 tablespoons breadcrumbs
Chopped parsley
Chopped mint
2 anchovies (chopped)
3 olives (chopped)

oil
1 kilo potatoes (sliced)
2 onions (sliced)
4 tomatoes cut in halves
3 cloves garlic

Method

Mix the breadcrumbs with the parsley, mint, anchovies and olives and bind with some oil. Put this mixture in the side of the fish and secure well with thread. Lay the sliced onions at the bottom of a well greased oven dish, cover with the sliced potatoes and place the prepared fish on top. Cover with the tomato halves, add the mint then sprinkle with salt, pepper and oil. Bake in a moderate oven for 1½ hours.

LAMPUKI
WITH PIQUANT SAUCE
(LAMPUKI BIZ-ZALZA)

Serves 4

Ingredients

1 kilo lampuki
A knob of margerine (melted)
Seasoning
4 olives (chopped)
1 tablespoon capers
1 onion (chopped)
100g mushrooms (chopped)

1 green pepper
25g seasoned flour
4 tomatoes
150ml water or fish stock
Olive oil
1 teaspoon paprika

Method

Place the lampuki in a baking dish. Brush with melted margerine and sprinkle with salt and pepper. Pour in the water or fish stock. Cover with greased paper and bake in a moderate oven for 15 minutes. Remove from the oven and retain the stock for the sauce. Heat the olive oil and brown the onions, mushrooms and pepper. Add the flour, tomatoes, seasoning, paprika, olives, capers and stock. Bring to the boil and cook for about 5 minutes. Pour over the fish and serve with salad and chips.

FRIED LAMPUKI
(LAMPUKI MOQLIJA)

Serves 4

Ingredients

1 kilo lampuki
Seasoned flour

Olive oil

Method
Coat the slices of lampuki in seasoned flour. Heat the oil and fry the lampuki until golden brown.
Serve with salad and chips.

STEWED OCTOPUS
(STUFFAT TAL-QARNIT)

Serves 4

Ingredients

1 large octopus
200g tomato paste
2 large onions
Olive oil

6 olives cut into pieces
½ kilo tomatoes
1 spoonful capers

Method
Beat and fry the octopus. In a separate saucepan, brown the onions in some olive oil; add the diluted tomato paste and the tomatoes. Cook until the tomatoes are tender. Add the fried octopus, the olives and the capers. Cook for about 1 hour. Serve the sauce with spaghetti.

WHITE BAIT
(MAKKU)

Serves 4-6

Ingredients
1 kilo white bait
3 well beaten eggs
Parsley

1 clove garlic (crushed)
Olive oil
Seasoning

Method
Mix the white bait with the well beaten eggs, add the garlic, parsley and seasoning. Heat the olive oil and fry the white bait on a gentle heat until the mass is brown. Serve with salad and chips.

BAKED TUNNY
(TONN IL-FORN)

Serves 4

Ingredients
1 kilo fresh tunny
36 kilo sliced potatoes
4 cloves garlic
½ kilo tomatoes (halves)
3 sliced onions

1 tablespoon vinegar
Seasoning
Mint
Parsley
Olive oil
150ml water

Method
Place the sliced onions at the bottom of a well greased oven dish. Lay the sliced potatoes on top of the onions and place the fish in the centre of the dish. Cover with the tomato halves, add the garlic, vinegar, seasoning, mint, parsley, olive oil and water. Bake in a moderately hot oven for about 1 hour.

Sweets

ST. MARTIN'S CAKE
(TRADITIONAL CAKE FOR SAN MARTIN)
(11 NOVEMBER)

Ingredients

400g flour
200g sugar
200g butter
4 eggs
4 tablespoons milk
1 tablespoon mixed spice

200g walnuts (chopped)
200g hazelnuts (chopped)
100g almonds (chopped)
100g figs (chopped)
100g chestnuts (chopped)
and roasted)

Method

Cream the butter and sugar until soft and fluffy. Add beaten eggs and fold in the flour and spice. Add the nuts and figs and put the mixture in a well garnished dish. Bake for 1½ hours or until golden brown.

VITTORIN
(TRADITIONAL SWEET FOR THE FEAST OF IL-VITTORJA)
(8 SEPTEMBER)

Ingredients
400g flaky pastry
200g jam
Juice of 1 lemon
Grated rind of 1 lemon
200g breadcrumbs

Method
Mix the jam with the juice and rind of the lemon. Add the breadcrumbs. Grease a dish with fat and line the bottom and sides with the pastry. Put the jam mixture in the dish. Roll out pastry and cut into thin strips and form a trellis on the jam mixture. Bake in a moderate oven until golden brown.

PRINJOLATA
(TRADITIONAL CARNIVAL SWEET)

Ingredients
1 sponge cake
100g almonds (chopped)
100g cherries
100g candied peel
100g dark chocolate (melted)

Ingredients for butter cream:
200g butter
150g icing sugar (sieved)
½ teaspoon vanilla essence
100g almonds (chopped)

Method
Cream the butter until very soft and white; it is essential not to warm it. Gradually work in sugar and vanilla flavouring. Add chopped almonds. Cut sponge cake into slices.

Lightly grease a pudding basin with butter, alternate sponge cake and butter cream and leave overnight to set. Remove from basin and decorate with almonds, cherries, candied peel and melted chocolate.

DEAD MAN'S BONES
(TRADITIONAL SWEETS FOR ALL SOULS' DAY)
(2 NOVEMBER)

Ingredients
2 egg whites
Few drops almond essence
150g castor sugar
150g ground almonds
Icing sugar

Method
Whisk the egg whites until very stiff. Add the almond essence, then add the sugar and ground almonds. Shape the mixture into leg bones and bake in the centre of a moderate oven for 20 minutes. Sprinkle some icing sugar on top.

CHESTNUTS PURÉE
(IMBULJUTA)

Ingredients

400g dried chestnuts
Rind of 1 tangerine
Rind of 1 orange
Rind of 1 lemon

½ teaspoon mixed spice
1 teaspoon cloves
100g cocoa powder
200g brown sugar

Method

Peel the dried chestnuts and soak overnight. Put all ingredients in a deep pot; cover with water and bring to the boil. Simmer until the chestnuts are very tender. Serve hot.

DATE SLICES
(IMQARET)

Ingredients

Pastry:
200g flour
25g lard
25g margerine
25g sugar
1 tablespoon anisette
1 tablespoon orange flower
water

Filling:
200g dates
1 tablespoon anisette
1 tablespoon orange flower
water
Grated rind of 1 lemon
Grated rind of 1 orange
Grated rind of 1 tangerine
½ teaspoon mixed spice

Method

Pastry: Mix all ingredients and knead into a smooth dough. Let the dough stand for 30 minutes.

Filling: Mix all ingredients and simmer until the mixture is smooth. Roll out pastry into long strips and put some mixture in the middle and lay another strip over the mixture. Press ends and sides. Cut into rhombus shapes and deep fry until golden brown.

ST. JOSEPH'S BUNS
(SFINEĠ TA' SAN ĠUŻEPP)

Ingredients

Buns:
200g flour
100g sugar
2 tablespoons baking powder
Pinch of salt
25g margerine
1 egg
150ml milk
Fat for deep frying

Filling:
400g rikotta
50g sugar
50g chopped chocolate
50g chopped candied peel
50g chopped cherries
Juice of 1 orange
½ teaspoon vanilla
1 tablespoon brandy

Method

Sieve the flour, baking powder and salt. Rub in margarine. Add the egg and enough milk to form a dough, roll into balls and deep fry until golden brown. Drain on absorbent paper.

Combine all ingredients and slit the buns and fill with the rikotta mixture. Dip in syrup.

RIKOTTA TUBES
(KANNOLI TAR-RIKOTTA)

Ingredients

Pastry:
400g flour
2 egg yolks
3 tablespoons lard
3 tablespoons sugar
½ teaspoon vanilla
Some brandy

Filling:
40g rikotta
50g sugar

4 bars of dark chocolate
   (chopped)
50g candied peel (chopped)
Pinch of cinnamon
Juice of 1 tangerine
   or orange
4 glace cherries
   (chopped)
½ teaspoon vanilla
50g almonds (chopped)
Icing sugar

Method

Mix well the sugar and flour, add the lard.

Add the yolks, vanilla and enough brandy to form a stiff dough. Let the dough stand for 30 minutes.

Roll out the pastry into thin strips and wind round especially prepared tin tubes.

Deep fry in hot oil until golden brown. Rid off any excess oil by using kitchen paper.

Let the tubes cool, then slide off the tin tubes.

Mix all ingredients except icing sugar. Fill pastry cases with the mixture and roll in icing sugar.

STUFFED DATES
(TAMAL MIMLI)

Ingredients

½ kilo dates
100g round almonds
50g icing sugar
50g castor sugar

Few drops almond essence
Egg yolk to mix
Food colouring

Method

Remove the stones from dates. Make filling by mixing rest of the ingredients, adding enough egg yolk to make a firm mixture. Knead thoroughly. Fill each date with a small quantity of the almond paste. Sprinkle some icing sugar on top of the dates.

PANCAKES STUFFED WITH RIKOTTA
(PANCAKES MIMLIJA BIR-RIKOTTA)

Ingredients

Filling:
400g rikotta
50g almonds (chopped)
Bar of dark chocolate (chopped)
50g cherries (chopped)
50g candied peel
100g sugar

Pancakes:
200g plain flour
Pinch of salt
2 eggs
300ml milk
50g castor sugar
A grating of lemon rind
Honey

Method

Thoroughly mix the rikotta with the rest of the ingredients. Set aside. Sieve the flour and salt, add the egg yolks and beat in about half the milk. Whisk thoroughly to aerate the mixture, then add the remaining milk. Whisk the egg whites until stiff, whisk in the sugar and lemon rind and fold this mixture into the batter. Cook by heating a little butter in a frying pan and pouring in just enough butter mixture to cover the bottom of the pan. Cook the

pancake until brown on the under-side, then loosen the edges, shake it down into the curve of the pan and toss or turn it with a palette knife. Brown other side and turn it on to a paper dredged with castor sugar. Fill the pancakes with the rikotta mixture, roll and sprinkle with honey.

STUFFED PRUNES

(PRUNA MIMLIJA)

Ingredients

½ kilo prunes
200g coconut
Few drops vanilla essence

½ tin condensed milk
Food colouring
Walnut halves

Method

Stone the prunes. Mix the coconut with the vanilla essence and the condensed milk. Stuff the prunes with the coconut mixture and top with walnut halves.

DOUGHNOUTS
(BAMBOLONI)

Ingredients

15g fresh yeast
50g sugar
150ml tepid water
350g flour

Pinch of salt
25g margerine
Oil for deep frying
Jam

Method

Cream the yeast with 1 teaspoon of the sugar. Add the tepid water and a sprinkling of flour. Let yeast mixture stand for 30 minutes. Sieve flour and salt into a bowl, rub in margerine and add rest of the sugar. Add the yeast liquid and knead thoroughly. Put in a warm place for at least 1 hour, until doubled in size. Form dough into balls and deep fry until golden brown. Top with jam and sugar.

TREACLE RINGS
(QAGHAQ TA' L-GHASEL)

Ingredients

Pastry:
400g flour
100g semolina
200g margerine
100g sugar
1 egg yolk
Milk to bind

Filling:
400g black treacle
400g sugar
2 tablespoons anisette
Grated rind of orange
Grated rind of lemon
4 cloves
2 teaspoons semolina
3 teaspoons anisette
1 teaspoon mixed spice
150ml water

Method

Mix the flour with the semolina, margarine and sugar. Add the yolk and milk. Knead well until the pastry is quite smooth.

Mix the treacle with the sugar, cocoa, orange and lemon rind, cloves, anisette, spice and water. Put in a saucepan and simmer until the mass thickens. Then gradually add the semolina. Remove from the heat and let the mixture cool. Roll out pastry into long thin strips; put some mixture in the middle, roll pastry to form long tubes. Form each tube into a ring, cut slits with a sharp knife and bake until golden brown.

KWAREŻIMAL
(LENTAL SWEET)

Ingredients

400g ground almonds
200g flour
200g ground rice
water
400g brown sugar
1 teaspoon mixed spice
1 tablespoon cocoa

Grated rind of 1 lemon
Grated rind of 1 orange
1 teaspoon orange flower
Milk to bind ingredients
Honey and pistacchio nuts
(chopped) for topping

Method

Thoroughly mix all ingredients and form a stiff paste by binding with the milk. Roll out pastry and cut into oblong pieces; put on a well greased baking dish and bake until golden brown. Let cool, then top with honey and chopped pistacchio nuts.

FIGOLLI
(TRADITIONAL EASTER SWEETS)

Ingredients

Pastry:
1 kilo plain flour
400g margerine
400g sugar
2 egg yolks
Water to mix

Glace Icing:
400g icing sugar
3 desertspoon warm water

Filling:
200g ground almonds
100g icing sugar
100g castor sugar
Few drops almond essence
2 egg yolks to mix
Jam

Method

Make pastry by sieving the flour and rubbing in butter lightly. Add sugar and mix with egg yolk and water. Knead very lightly on floured board. Let the pastry stand for 1 hour. Roll out pastry and cut the figolli by using various steps (mermaid, duck, horse etc). Bake in a moderate hot oven until golden brown.

Make the filling by mixing the ground almonds with the icing sugar, castor sugar and almond essence. Add the egg yolks to make a firm mixture. Knead thoroughly. Take two figolli of the same shape, cover the bottom one with jam and put a layer of the almond mixture on top. Cover with the other identical shape. Decorate the figolli with glace icing and a small Easter egg.

BREAD AND BUTTER PUDDING
(PUDINA TAL-ĦOBŻ BIL-BUTIR)

Ingredients
2 eggs
1 level teaspoon sugar
450ml milk

6 large slices bread with butter
50g currants

Method
Beat the eggs with a fork. Add the sugar and milk. Remove the crusts from the bread and cut into squares. Place in a greased oven proof dish and sprinkle over the currants. Pour in the beaten egg mixture; sprinkle a little sugar over the top. Allow to stand for 30 minutes and bake in a moderate oven for 1 hour. Serve cold.

BREAD PUDDING
(PUDINA TAL-ĦOBŻ)

Ingredients
1 kilo bread (minus crust)
600ml milk
1 tablespoon grated orange peel
1 tablespoon grated lemon peel
50g sugar
2 eggs
25g margarine

1 tablespoon custard
  powder
200g sultana
50g candied peel
1 tablespoon cocoa
1 tablespoon vanilla
100g coconut

Method
Soak bread in milk. Add the margerine, orange peel, lemon peel and sugar. Mix well. Add the rest of the ingredients except eggs. Beat the eggs and add to the mixture. Put in a well greased oven dish and bake for 1 hour or until golden brown. Serve cold.

APPLE PUDDING
(PUDINA TAT-TUFFIEĦ)

Ingredients
1 kilo apples
½ kilo breadcrumbs

100g sugar
100g candied peel
4 eggs

Method
Peel and core apples. Cut into quarters; then cut each quarter into three pieces. Mix with the rest of the dry ingredients. Add the well beaten eggs. Butter a pudding basin, place the mixture in the bowl, cover with grease-proof paper and napkin. Boil for 1½ hours.